The Art of
Bread Baking

A Collection of Delicious Recipes
Bread Machine and Oven Friendly

Alec Richter

Copyright © 2023 - All rights reserved.

The content contained within this book may not be reproduced, duplicated, or transmitted without direct written permission from the author or the publisher.

Under no circumstances will any blame or legal responsibility be held against the publisher, or author, for any damages, reparation, or monetary loss due to the information contained within this book. Either directly or indirectly.

Legal Notice: This book is copyright protected. This book is only for personal use. You cannot amend, distribute, sell, use, quote, or paraphrase any part, or the content within this book, without the consent of the author or publisher.

Disclaimer Notice: Please note the information contained within this document is for educational and entertainment purposes only. All effort has been executed to present accurate, up-to-date, and reliable, complete information. No warranties of any kind are declared or implied. Readers acknowledge that the author is not engaging in the rendering of legal, financial, medical, or professional advice. The content within this book has been derived from various sources. Please consult a licensed professional before attempting any techniques outlined in this book.

By reading this document, the reader agrees that under no circumstances is the author responsible for any losses, direct or indirect, which are incurred as a result of the use of the information contained within this document, including, but not limited to, — errors, omissions, or inaccuracies.

Table of Contents

Introduction	6
Chapter 1: History of Bread	7
Chapter 2: What Types of Bread Are?	8
Chapter 3: Easiest Way To Start Baking Bread?	9
Chapter 4: Main Ingredients	10
Chapter 5: Main Tools	11
Chapter 6: The Basics of Kneading and Fermenting	12
Chapter 7: What to Choose: A Regular Oven Or Bread Machine?	13
1. Regular Oven:	13
2. Bread Machine:	13
Chapter 8: Bread Recipes	15
Basic Breads	*15*
Bread Machine White Bread	16
Basic White Bread	17
Whole Wheat Bread	18
Bread Machine Whole Wheat Bread	19
Bread Machine Multi Grain Loaf	20
Artisan Bread	21
Pita Bread	22
Rustic Sourdough Bread	24
Herbed Focaccia Bread	24
Sourdough Bread	26
Focaccia Bread	27
Rosemary & Sea Salt Focaccia	28
Garlic & Herb Dinner Rolls	29
Oatmeal Honey Bread	30

Rustic Italian Bread ... 31

Traditional Breads ... *32*
Bread Machine Flax and Sunflower Seed Bread ... 33
Bread Machine Sour Cream and Poppy Seed Bread ... 34
Oatmeal Bread ... 35
Multi-Seed Bread ... 36
Rosemary and Olive oil Bread ... 37

Italian Breads ... *39*
Challah ... 40
Salty Italian Bread ... 41
Rosemary and Garlic Focaccia Bread ... 42
Bread Machine Ciabatta ... 44
Pagnotta ... 45

French Breads ... *47*
French Baguettes ... 48
Garlic and Herb Bread ... 49
Country French Bread ... 50
French Spiced Bread ... 52
Tarte Flambee ... 53
Rye Bread ... 54

Fruits and Nuts Breads ... *57*
Bread Machine Banana Bread ... 58
Bread Machine Apple Chunk Bread ... 59
Bread Machine Walnut and Raisin Loaf ... 60
Cranberry Bread ... 61
Lemon and Blueberry Bread ... 62

Sweet Breads ... *64*
Bread Machine Molasses Bread ... 65
Cinnamon and Sugar Bread ... 66
Lemon Cake Bread ... 67
Cinnamon Raisin Bread ... 68
Stollen ... 69

Bonus Recipes! Pizza	*72*
Pepperoni Pizza	73
Margherita Pizza	74
Red Onions and Mushroom Pizza	75
Conclusion	**77**

Introduction

Welcome to the world of bread baking! This cookbook brings together a collection of classic and innovative bread recipes, each with its own unique flavor and texture. From crusty baguettes to soft sandwich loaves, there's a bread for every occasion. So, put on your apron, grab your ingredients, and let's get baking!"

Chapter 1:
History of Bread

Bread has been a staple food for thousands of years and has a rich history that dates back to ancient civilizations. The earliest evidence of bread making dates back to ancient Egypt around 5000 BC, where the grains of wheat were ground into flour and mixed with water to form a dough. Over time, bread making techniques spread throughout the world and different cultures added their own unique ingredients and flavors to create a wide variety of breads. Today, bread continues to be a staple food in many cultures and is enjoyed in many forms, from simple slices of white bread to artisanal loaves made with complex combinations of grains and flavors.

Chapter 2:
What Types of Bread Are?

There are many different types of bread, including:

1. **Sourdough** - A tangy, fermented bread made with a natural yeast culture.
2. **Rye** - A dense, flavorful bread made with rye flour and often mixed with wheat flour.
3. **Whole grain** - A bread made with a mixture of whole grains, including wheat, oats, barley, and cornmeal.
4. **Focaccia** - An Italian flatbread that is typically topped with olive oil and salt.
5. **Ciabatta** - A soft, airy Italian bread that is perfect for sandwiches.
6. **Baguette** - A long, thin French bread with a crispy crust.
7. **Naan** - A soft, pillowy flatbread from India that is traditionally baked in a tandoor oven.
8. **Pita** - A round, pocket bread that is often filled with falafel, hummus, or other fillings.
9. **Brioche** - A rich, buttery bread that is commonly used to make sweet pastries.
10. **Multigrain** - A bread made with a mixture of different grains, including wheat, corn, and flax.

These are just a few examples of the many different types of bread available. Each type of bread has its own unique flavor, texture, and history.

Chapter 3:
Easiest Way To Start Baking Bread?

Starting to bake bread can seem intimidating, but with a few simple tips, you can be on your way to creating delicious homemade bread in no time! Here are some steps to get you started:

1. **Choose a simple recipe:** Start with a basic bread recipe, such as a white or whole wheat bread, that doesn't require any special ingredients or techniques.
2. **Gather your ingredients:** You will need flour, yeast, salt, and water. You may also want to add sugar or oil to enhance the flavor of your bread.
3. **Mix the dough:** Combine the ingredients in a large mixing bowl and knead the dough for about 10 minutes until it is smooth and elastic.
4. **Let the dough rise:** Place the dough in a greased bowl, cover it with plastic wrap, and let it rise in a warm, draft-free place for about an hour or until it has doubled in size.
5. **Shape the dough:** Punch down the dough and shape it into a loaf or rolls.
6. **Bake the bread:** Place the shaped dough in a greased loaf pan or on a baking sheet and bake in a preheated oven at 375°F (190°C) for 30-40 minutes, or until the bread is golden brown.
7. **Enjoy your bread:** Once the bread has cooled, slice and serve with your favorite toppings, such as butter or jam.

By following these steps, you will have a basic understanding of how to make bread from scratch, and you can then experiment with different recipes and ingredients to find your perfect bread.

Chapter 4:
Main Ingredients

The main ingredients in bread are flour, yeast, salt, and water. These ingredients form the basic structure of bread and can be adjusted to create different types of bread with different textures, flavors, and aromas. Other common ingredients in bread include sugar, oil, and eggs, which can be added to enhance the flavor, texture, and color of the bread. Some bread recipes also call for other ingredients such as honey, milk, cheese, or fruit. These ingredients can be used to create sweet or savory breads, and can be added in a variety of combinations to create unique and delicious breads.

Chapter 5:
Main Tools

Here are the basic tools you'll need for baking bread:

1. **Mixing bowl:** A large bowl for mixing the dough.
2. **Measuring cups and spoons:** For accurately measuring the ingredients.
3. **Wooden spoon or spatula:** For mixing and kneading the dough.
4. **Dough scraper:** For dividing and shaping the dough.
5. **Baking sheet or loaf pan:** For baking the bread.
6. **Oven:** For baking the bread.
7. **Kitchen scale:** For measuring ingredients by weight, which is more accurate than measuring by volume.
8. **Proofing basket (optional):** For letting the dough rise.
9. **Instant-read thermometer (optional):** For checking the internal temperature of the bread.

By having these basic tools on hand, you'll be able to bake bread with ease and consistency. As you gain experience and confidence in bread baking, you may choose to invest in additional tools such as a stand mixer or a bread machine.

Chapter 6:
The Basics of Kneading and Fermenting

Kneading and fermenting are two crucial steps in making bread.

1. **Kneading:** Kneading is the process of mixing and working the dough to develop the gluten strands. This creates a network of gluten strands that will give the bread its structure and texture. Kneading can be done by hand, using a stand mixer with a dough hook, or in a bread machine. Kneading usually takes about 10 minutes by hand, or 5-8 minutes with a stand mixer.
2. **Fermenting:** Fermenting is the process of allowing the yeast in the dough to grow and multiply. This creates carbon dioxide gas, which makes the dough rise and become light and airy. Fermenting typically takes about an hour, although this can vary depending on the recipe and the conditions in your kitchen.

Both kneading and fermenting are essential to making great bread, so it's important to take the time to do them properly. By following the instructions in your recipe and paying close attention to the dough as it comes together, you'll be able to make delicious, crusty, and fluffy bread every time!

Chapter 7:
What to Choose: A Regular Oven Or Bread Machine?

The choice between using a regular oven or a bread machine ultimately depends on your personal preference and baking habits. Here are some pros and cons of each option to help you decide:

1. Regular Oven:

Pros:

- You have complete control over the baking process and can make adjustments as needed.
- You can bake a wider variety of breads, including sourdough and other artisan breads, in a regular oven.
- Baking bread in a regular oven can be a fun and rewarding experience that allows you to connect with the baking process and learn new skills.

Cons:

- Baking bread in a regular oven requires more time and effort, as you need to mix, knead, and shape the dough yourself.
- You'll need to be careful when checking the bread during baking to avoid burning yourself or the bread.

2. Bread Machine:

Pros:

- A bread machine does the work of mixing, kneading, and fermenting for you, making bread making a lot easier and

faster.
- Bread machines are great for busy bakers who don't have a lot of time to spend in the kitchen.
- They produce consistent results every time and make it easy to make different types of breads with different ingredients.

Cons:

- Bread machines are limited in the types of breads they can make. They typically make bread with a softer texture and a mild flavor.
- They can be bulky and take up a lot of counter space.
- They can be expensive, especially high-end models.

In conclusion, if you're looking for an easy and convenient way to make bread, a bread machine may be the right choice for you. But if you're passionate about baking and want to learn new skills, a regular oven will allow you to do that.

Chapter 8:
Bread Recipes

Basic Breads

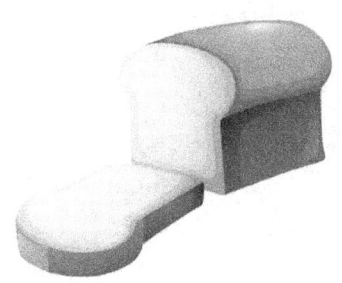

Bread Machine White Bread

Preparation Time: 2 hours and 20 minutes | Cooking Time: 40 minutes| Servings: 12

Ingredients:

- 3 cups all-purpose bread flour, unbleached
- 2 tablespoons white sugar
- 0.25 ounce of bread machine yeast
- 1 teaspoon salt
- 1 cup water, at 110 degrees F or 45 degrees C
- 1/4 cup vegetable oil

Directions

1. Take a bread machine, add ingredients according to the manufacturer's instructions or place yeast and sugar in its pan.
2. Pour in water, stir lightly and let it rest for 10 minutes until the mixture turns foamy.
3. After 10 minutes, add salt and bread flour to the yeast mixture, and pour in the oil.
4. Plug in the bread machine, press the setting for "basic" or "white bread," set the crust color to "light" or "medium," and then press start and let it bake.
5. When the bread cycle is done, take out the pan and then let the bread loaf rest in the pan for 5 minutes.
6. Then transfer the bread loaf to a wire rack and let it cool completely.
7. When ready to eat, cut the bread loaf into slices and then serve.

Nutritional Information Per Serving:

Calories: 174 Cal; Total Fats: 5 g; Saturated Fat: 1 g; Carbohydrate: 27 g; Sugar: 2 g; Fiber: 1 g; Protein: 4 g

Basic White Bread

Preparation Time: 2 hours and 30 minutes (includes rising time)

Ingredients:

- 3 cups all-purpose flour
- 1 teaspoon salt
- 1 teaspoon sugar
- 1 packet of active dry yeast
- 1 1/2 cups warm water
- 2 tablespoons olive oil

Directions:

1. In a large mixing bowl, combine the flour, salt, and sugar.
2. In a separate bowl, dissolve the yeast in warm water. Let stand for 5 minutes until the mixture becomes frothy.
3. Add the yeast mixture and olive oil to the flour mixture and stir until a dough forms.
4. Turn the dough out onto a floured surface and knead for 10 minutes until the dough is smooth and elastic.
5. Place the dough in a lightly oiled bowl, cover with a damp cloth, and let it rise in a warm place for 1 hour.
6. Preheat the oven to 425°F (220°C).
7. Transfer the dough to a greased loaf pan and let it rise for another 30 minutes.
8. Bake the bread in the preheated oven for 30-35 minutes, or until the crust is golden brown.
9. Let the bread cool in the pan for 5 minutes before removing it from the pan and letting it cool completely on a wire rack.

Nutritional Information Per Serving (1 slice):

Calcium: 40 mg, Carbohydrates: 28 g, Cholesterol: 0 mg, Fat: 2 g, Fiber: 1 g, Protein: 3 g, Sodium: 220 mg

★★★★★

Whole Wheat Bread

Preparation Time: 2 hours and 30 minutes (includes rising time)

Ingredients:

- 3 cups whole wheat flour
- 1 teaspoon salt
- 1 teaspoon honey
- 1 packet of active dry yeast
- 1 1/2 cups warm water
- 2 tablespoons melted butter

Directions:

1. In a large mixing bowl, combine the flour, salt, and honey.
2. In a separate bowl, dissolve the yeast in warm water. Let stand for 5 minutes until the mixture becomes frothy.
3. Add the yeast mixture and melted butter to the flour mixture and stir until a dough forms.
4. Turn the dough out onto a floured surface and knead for 10 minutes until the dough is smooth and elastic.
5. Place the dough in a lightly oiled bowl, cover with a damp cloth, and let it rise in a warm place for 1 hour.
6. Preheat the oven to 425°F (220°C).
7. Transfer the dough to a greased loaf pan and let it rise for another 30 minutes.
8. Bake the bread in the preheated oven for 35-40 minutes, or until the crust is golden brown.
9. Let the bread cool in the pan for 5 minutes before removing it from the pan and letting it cool completely on a wire rack.

Nutritional Information Per Serving (1 slice):

Calories: 140, Fat: 4 g, Sodium: 220 mg, Carbohydrates: 24 g, Fiber: 4 g, Protein: 4 g, Cholesterol: 10 mg, Calcium: 40 mg

Bread Machine Whole Wheat Bread

Preparation Time: 3 hours and 10 minutes | Cooking Time: 1 hour and 15 minutes| Servings: 18

Ingredients:
- 3 1/2 cups white whole wheat flour, unbleached, sifted, leveled
- 1/4 cup sesame seeds
- 1 1/2 teaspoons salt
- 1 tablespoon vital wheat gluten
- 1 1/2 teaspoon instant yeast
- 1/4 cup honey
- 2 tablespoons olive oil
- 1 1/4 cups water, lukewarm

Directions
1. Plug in a bread machine, add ingredients according to the manufacturer's instructions, or pour water, oil, and honey into its pan.
2. Add whole wheat flour, sesame seeds, wheat gluten, salt, and yeast, and press the setting for "basic" or "whole wheat bread."
3. Set the crust color to "light" or "medium," then press start and let it bake.
4. When the bread cycle is done, take out the pan and let the bread loaf rest in the pan for 5 minutes.
5. Then transfer the bread loaf to a wire rack and let it cool completely.
6. When ready to eat, cut the bread loaf into slices and then serve.

Nutritional Information Per Serving:

Calories: 120 Cal; Total Fats: 5 g; Saturated Fat: 1 g; Carbohydrate: 21 g; Sugar: 4 g; Fiber: 3 g; Protein: 4 g

★★★★★

Bread Machine Multi Grain Loaf

Preparation Time: 10 minutes | Cooking Time: 3 hours and 30 minutes| Servings: 12

Ingredients:
- 1 1/3 cups all-purpose bread flour, unbleached, sifted, leveled
- 3 tablespoons brown sugar
- 1 1/2 cups whole-wheat flour, sifted, leveled
- 1 1/4 teaspoon salt
- 1 cup multi-grain cereal, uncooked
- 2 tablespoons butter, unsalted, softened
- 2 1/2 teaspoon bread machine yeast
- 1 1/4 cup water, at 110 degrees F or 45 degrees C

Directions
1. Take a bread machine, add ingredients according to the manufacturer's instructions or place yeast and brown sugar in it.
2. Pour in water, stir lightly and let it rest for 10 minutes until the mixture turns foamy.
3. After 10 minutes, add salt along with the remaining ingredients into the yeast mixture, plug in the bread machine and then press the setting for "basic" or "white bread."
4. Set the crust color to "light" or "medium," then press start and let it bake.
5. When the bread cycle is done, take out the pan and then let the bread loaf rest in the pan for 5 minutes.
6. Then transfer the bread loaf to a wire rack and let it cool completely.
7. When ready to eat, cut the bread loaf into slices and then serve.

Nutritional Information Per Serving:
Calories: 170 Cal; Total Fats: 2.5 g; Saturated Fat: 1.5 g; Carbohydrate: 31 g; Sugar: 4 g; Fiber: 4 g; Protein: 5 g

★★★★★

Artisan Bread

Preparation Time: 4 hours or more | Cooking Time: 25 minutes | Servings: 2

Ingredients:

- 3 1/4 cups bread flour, unbleached, sifted, leveled
- 2 teaspoons salt
- 2 teaspoons instant yeast
- 1 1/2 cups water, chilled
- Cornmeal as needed for the pan

Directions

1. Take a large mixing bowl, add flour, and then whisk in salt and yeast until combined.
2. Pour water into the flour mixture and then stir with a wooden spoon or a plastic spatula until well combined and the flour has turned moist and sticky; use your hands if needed.
3. Shape the dough into a ball, cover it with foil or a plastic wrap tightly and let it rest for 2 to 3 hours at room temperature until double in size.
4. Then transfer the covered dough bowl into the refrigerator and let it rest for a minimum of 18 hours or 3 days; the dough may rise and deflate after 2 days.
5. Take a large non-stick baking sheet, and dust it lightly with cornmeal.
6. Wipe clean a working space, dust it with flour and then place the cold bread dough on it.
7. Divide the dough into two pieces using a knife or scraper, and then place each of the dough pieces on the prepared baking sheet.
8. Shape each dough piece into a long 9-by-3 inches loaf using

floured hands, cover the tray loosely and let it rest for 45 minutes.
9. Meanwhile, switch on the oven, set it to 475 degrees F, and let it preheat.
10. After 45 minutes, uncover the bread loaf, and if it flattens out, shape the loaves again along the sides using floured hands.
11. Make three 1/2-inch deep slashes on top of each loaf, transfer the baking tray with the two scored bread doughs into the oven and then let it bake for 20 to 25 minutes until the top turns golden brown.
12. When done, gently tap each loaf, and if it sounds hollow, then the loaves are baked; otherwise, continue baking them for 5 more minutes.
13. When done, let the loaves cool on the wire rack for 5 minutes and then slice to serve.

Nutritional Information Per Serving:

Calories: 290 Cal; Total Fats: 4 g; Saturated Fat: 0.5 g; Carbohydrate: 55 g; Sugar: 8 g; Fiber: 3 g; Protein: 11 g

★★★★★

Pita Bread

Preparation Time: 2 hours minutes | Cooking Time: 15 minutes| Servings: 10

Ingredients:

- 3 1/2 cups all-purpose flour, unbleached
- 1 teaspoon salt
- 1 1/2 teaspoon instant yeast
- 1 teaspoon white sugar
- 2 tablespoons olive oil
- 1 1/2 cup water, at room temperature

Directions

1. Take a large bowl, place flour in it, add salt, sugar, and yeast, and then stir until combined.
2. Pour in the oil and water, and stir well until a well-combined and moist, and sticky dough comes together.
3. Wipe clean a working surface, grease it with oil, place dough on it and knead it for 5 to 8 minutes until elastic.
4. Cover the dough with a bowl, let it rest for 5 minutes, and then knead it again for 2 to 3 minutes until smooth and non-sticky.
5. Return the kneaded dough to its bowl, cover it with your towel and let it rest for 1 hour or more until doubled in size.
6. Then dust the working space with flour, place dough on it, roll it in a log shape, and cut it into evenly sized 10 pieces using a knife or scraper.
7. Brush the top of the dough pieces lightly with oil and cover them loosely with plastic wrap.
8. Working on one dough piece at a time, flatten it, fold and then shape it into a ball.
9. Cover the dough balls with plastic wrap for 30 minutes, and then use a rolling pin to roll each dough piece into a 6-inch dough circle.
10. Cover the dough circles and let them rest for another 10 minutes.
11. When ready to cook, switch on the oven, set it to 450 degrees F, and let it preheat.
12. Take a large baking sheet, place four pita dough circles on it, and then bake them for 5 minutes.
13. Bake the remaining pita breads in the same manner and then let them cool on a wire rack for 10 minutes before serving.

Nutritional Information Per Serving:

Calories: 205 Cal; Total Fats: 2.9 g; Saturated Fat: 0.7 g; Carbohydrate: 38.8 g; Sugar: 0.5 g; Fiber: 2 g; Protein: 5.4 g

★★★★★

Rustic Sourdough Bread

Preparation Time: 15 minutes + 2 days for fermenting

Ingredients:

- 1 cup sourdough starter
- 2 cups all-purpose flour
- 1 tsp salt
- 1 cup warm water

Directions:

1. In a large bowl, mix the sourdough starter, flour, salt and water.
2. Knead the dough for 10 minutes on a floured surface.
3. Place the dough in a greased bowl, cover with plastic wrap and let ferment for 24 hours in a warm place.
4. The next day, punch down the dough, knead for 5 minutes and let ferment for another 24 hours.
5. Preheat oven to 450°F and place a dutch oven inside to heat.
6. Shape the dough into a round loaf and place it into the preheated dutch oven.
7. Bake with the lid on for 30 minutes, then remove the lid and bake for another 10-15 minutes until golden brown.

Nutritional Information per Serving (1 slice):

Calories: 130, Fat: 1 g, Carbohydrates: 28 g, Protein: 4 g

Herbed Focaccia Bread

Preparation Time: 30 minutes + 2 hours rising time

Ingredients:

- 3 cups all-purpose flour
- 1 packet (7g) active dry yeast

- 1 tsp sugar
- 1 tsp salt
- 2 tbsp olive oil
- 1/2 cup warm water
- 2 tbsp fresh rosemary, chopped
- 1 tbsp fresh thyme, chopped
- 1 tsp garlic, minced

Directions:

1. In a large bowl, mix together the flour, yeast, sugar, and salt.
2. Add in the olive oil and warm water, and mix until a dough forms.
3. On a floured surface, knead the dough for 8-10 minutes.
4. Place the dough in a greased bowl, cover with plastic wrap and let it rise for 1 hour in a warm place.
5. Preheat your oven to 425°F.
6. On a floured surface, roll the dough out into a large rectangle. Place it on a greased baking sheet.
7. Use your fingers to make indentations all over the surface of the dough.
8. Sprinkle the rosemary, thyme, and garlic on top of the dough.
9. Bake in the oven for 20-25 minutes, or until the bread is golden brown.
10. Serve warm with olive oil and balsamic vinegar.

Nutritional Information Per Serving (1 slice, 1/12 of loaf):

Calories: 120kcal, Fat: 4g, Carbohydrates: 19g, Protein: 3g, Sodium: 300mg

Sourdough Bread

Preparation Time: 12-24 hours (including fermentation)

Ingredients:

- 500g all-purpose flour
- 400g water
- 100g sourdough starter
- 10g salt

Directions:

1. In a large bowl, mix together the flour, water and sourdough starter until well combined.
2. Cover the bowl with a cloth and let it rest for about 8-12 hours at room temperature.
3. Add salt to the mixture and knead it for 5-10 minutes until a smooth dough forms.
4. Place the dough in a floured bowl, cover it with a cloth, and let it rise for another 4-6 hours.
5. Preheat the oven to 230°C (450°F) and place a Dutch oven inside.
6. Place the dough into the Dutch oven, cover it and bake for 30 minutes.
7. Remove the lid and bake for an additional 20-25 minutes until the bread has a golden crust.
8. Allow the bread to cool completely on a wire rack before slicing.

Nutritional Information Per Serving (1 slice):

Calories: 150, Fat: 1g, Carbohydrates: 30g, Protein: 5g

★★★★★

Focaccia Bread

Preparation Time: 2 hours 30 minutes Ingredients:

- 2 1/2 cups all-purpose flour
- 1 tbsp active dry yeast
- 1 tsp sugar
- 1 tsp salt
- 1/2 cup warm water
- 1/4 cup olive oil
- Sea salt and fresh rosemary (optional)

Directions:

1. In a large mixing bowl, combine the flour, yeast, sugar, and salt.
2. Add in the warm water and olive oil and mix until the dough comes together.
3. Knead the dough for 5-10 minutes, until it is smooth and elastic.
4. Place the dough in a lightly oiled bowl, cover, and let it rise for 1 hour.
5. Preheat the oven to 425°F (220°C).
6. Place the dough on a lightly oiled baking sheet and press it out into a rectangle.
7. Brush the top of the dough with olive oil and sprinkle with sea salt and rosemary.
8. Bake the focaccia in the preheated oven for 15-20 minutes, or until the crust is golden brown.

Nutritional Information Per Serving: (1 slice)

Calories: 120, Fat: 6g, Carbs: 15g, Protein: 2g

★★★★★

Rosemary & Sea Salt Focaccia

Preparation Time: 15 minutes (plus 1 hour rising time) Servings: 8

Ingredients:

- 2 1/2 cups all-purpose flour
- 1/2 teaspoon active dry yeast
- 1 teaspoon sugar
- 1 teaspoon salt
- 1/2 teaspoon black pepper
- 1/3 cup olive oil
- 1/2 cup warm water
- 2 tablespoons chopped fresh rosemary
- 1 teaspoon sea salt

Directions:

1. In a large bowl, mix together the flour, yeast, sugar, salt, and black pepper.
2. Add the olive oil, warm water, and rosemary to the bowl and mix until a dough forms.
3. Turn the dough out onto a lightly floured surface and knead for 5 minutes.
4. Place the dough in a greased bowl and cover with plastic wrap. Let rise in a warm place for 1 hour.
5. Preheat oven to 425°F.
6. Place the dough on a lightly greased baking sheet. Flatten the dough into a round shape and sprinkle with the sea salt.
7. Bake for 20-25 minutes, or until the focaccia is golden brown.

Nutritional Information Per Serving:

Calories: 350, Fat: 18g, Cholesterol: 0mg, Sodium: 600mg, Carbohydrates: 42g, Protein: 6g

★★★★★

Garlic & Herb Dinner Rolls

Preparation Time: 30 minutes (plus 1 hour rising time) Servings: 12

Ingredients:

- 2 cups all-purpose flour
- 1/4 teaspoon active dry yeast
- 1 teaspoon sugar
- 1/2 teaspoon salt
- 3 tablespoons unsalted butter, melted
- 1/2 cup warm milk
- 2 cloves garlic, minced
- 2 tablespoons chopped fresh parsley
- 1 tablespoon chopped fresh thyme

Directions:

1. In a large bowl, mix together the flour, yeast, sugar, and salt.
2. Add the melted butter, warm milk, garlic, parsley, and thyme to the bowl and mix until a dough forms.
3. Turn the dough out onto a lightly floured surface and knead for 5 minutes.
4. Place the dough in a greased bowl and cover with plastic wrap. Let rise in a warm place for 1 hour.
5. Preheat oven to 375°F.
6. Divide the dough into 12 equal pieces and shape into round rolls.
7. Place the rolls on a greased baking sheet and bake for 15-20 minutes, or until the rolls are golden brown.

Nutritional Information Per Serving:

Calories: 140, Fat: 6g, Cholesterol: 15mg, Sodium: 200mg, Carbohydrates: 19g, Protein: 3g

Oatmeal Honey Bread

Preparation Time: 20 minutes + 1 hour rising time Ingredients:

- 2 cups all-purpose flour
- 1 cup rolled oats
- 1 packet (7g) active dry yeast
- 2 tbsp honey
- 1 tsp salt
- 1/2 cup warm water
- 1/4 cup melted butter

Directions:

1. In a large bowl, mix together the flour, oats, yeast, honey, and salt.
2. Add in the warm water and melted butter, and mix until a dough forms.
3. On a floured surface, knead the dough for 8-10 minutes.
4. Place the dough in a greased bowl, cover with plastic wrap and let it rise for 1 hour in a warm place.
5. Preheat your oven to 425°F.
6. Grease a 9x5 inch loaf pan.
7. Place the dough in the loaf pan and let it rise for an additional 20 minutes.
8. Bake in the oven for 30-35 minutes, or until the bread is golden brown.
9. Remove the bread from the oven and let it cool completely.
10. Serve sliced and toasted, spread with butter and jam.

Nutritional Information Per Serving (1 slice, 1/12 of loaf):

Calories: 170kcal, Fat: 7g, Carbohydrates: 25g, Protein: 4g, Sodium: 300mg

Rustic Italian Bread

Preparation Time: 10 minutes Active Time: 2 hours Total Time: 2 hours 10 minutes Servings: 12

Ingredients:

- 3 cups warm water
- 1 tbsp active dry yeast
- 2 tbsp salt
- 6 cups all-purpose flour
- 2 tbsp cornmeal

Directions:

1. In a large bowl, combine the warm water and yeast. Stir until the yeast is dissolved.
2. Add the salt to the yeast mixture and stir to combine.
3. Add the all-purpose flour, 1 cup at a time, until a dough forms.
4. Knead the dough on a floured surface for 10 minutes.
5. Place the dough in a greased bowl, cover with plastic wrap, and let it rise in a warm place for 1 hour.
6. Preheat the oven to 450°F.
7. Sprinkle a baking sheet with cornmeal.
8. Divide the dough into two pieces and shape into two rounds. Place the dough rounds onto the baking sheet.
9. Bake for 20 minutes, or until the bread is golden brown and sounds hollow when tapped.
10. Let the bread cool on a wire rack.

Nutritional Information Per Serving: Calories:

170 Fat: 0.5 g Protein: 5 g Carbs: 37 g Fiber: 2 g

★★★★★

Traditional Breads

Bread Machine Flax and Sunflower Seed Bread

Preparation Time: 10 minutes | Cooking Time: 1 hour and 50 minutes| Servings: 15

Ingredients:
- 1 1/2 cup bread flour, unbleached
- 1/2 cup flax seeds
- 1 teaspoon salt
- 1 1/3 cups whole-wheat flour, unbleached
- 1 teaspoon active dry yeast
- 3 tablespoons honey
- 1/2 cup sunflower seeds
- 1 1/3 cup water, at room temperature
- 2 tablespoons butter, unsalted, softened

Directions

1. Take a bread machine, add ingredients according to the manufacturer's instructions or add all the ingredients except for sunflower seeds into its pan.
2. Plug in the bread machine, press the "knead" setting and when done, sprinkle sunflower seeds over the dough.
3. Then select the "basic" or "whole wheat bread" cycle, set the crust color to "light" or "medium," and then press start and let it bake.
4. When the bread cycle is done, take out the pan and then let the bread loaf rest in the pan for 5 minutes.
5. Then transfer the bread loaf to a wire rack and let it cool completely.
6. When ready to eat, cut the bread loaf into slices and then serve.

Nutritional Information Per Serving:

Calories: 140 Cal; Total Fats: 4 g; Saturated Fat: 1 g; Carbohydrate: 23 g; Sugar: 4 g; Fiber: 3 g; Protein: 4 g

★★★★★

Bread Machine Sour Cream and Poppy Seed Bread

Preparation Time: 10 minutes | Cooking Time: 1 hour and 50 minutes | Servings: 12

Ingredients:

- 3 cups white whole-wheat flour
- 2 teaspoons dry yeast, active
- 1 teaspoon sea salt
- 2 tablespoons butter, unsalted, cut into pieces
- 4 teaspoons sugar
- 1 egg, at room temperature
- 1/2 cup water, at room temperature
- 1/2 teaspoon poppy seeds
- 1/2 cup sour cream, at room temperature

Directions

1. Plug in a bread machine, add ingredients according to the manufacturer's instructions, or add egg and then pour sour cream and water into its pan.
2. Add flour, salt, sugar, poppy seed, and yeast at the end and press the setting for "basic" or "white wheat bread."
3. Set the crust color to "light" or "medium," and then press start and let it bake.
4. When the bread cycle is done, take out the pan and then let the bread loaf rest in the pan
5. for 5 minutes.
6. Then transfer the bread loaf to a wire rack and let it cool completely.
7. When ready to eat, cut the bread loaf into slices and then serve.

Nutritional Information Per Serving:

Calories: 107.2 Cal; Total Fats: 4.8 g; Saturated Fat: 0.8 g; Carbohydrate: 13.7 g; Sugar: 7.2 g; Fiber: 0.2 g; Protein: 1.8 g

★★★★★

Oatmeal Bread

Preparation Time: 10 minutes | Cooking Time: 2 hours and 30 minutes | Servings: 12

Ingredients:

- 2 1/4 cups bread flour, unbleached
- 1 teaspoon bread machine yeast
- 1/4 cup brown sugar
- 3/4 cup old fashion oatmeal and more for sprinkling
- 1 teaspoon salt
- 3 tablespoons butter, unsalted, sliced
- 1 1/8 cup milk, lukewarm

Directions

1. Plug in a bread machine, add ingredients according to the manufacturer's instructions, or add butter and then pour the milk into its pan.
2. Add flour, sugar, oatmeal, salt, and yeast at the end and press the "knead" button.
3. When done, sprinkle some more oatmeal on top of the dough, select the setting for "basic" or "white wheat bread," let the crust color to "light" or "medium," then press start and let it bake.
4. When the bread cycle is done, take out the pan and then let the bread loaf rest in the pan for 5 minutes.
5. Then transfer the bread loaf to a wire rack and let it cool completely.

6. When ready to eat, cut the bread loaf into slices and then serve.

Nutritional Information Per Serving:

Calories: 73 Cal; Total Fats: 1.2 g; Saturated Fat: 0.2 g; Carbohydrate: 13 g; Sugar: 2.2 g; Fiber: 1.1 g; Protein: 2.3 g

★★★★★

Multi-Seed Bread

Preparation Time: 12 hours and 10 minutes | Cooking Time: 45 minutes| Servings: 12

Ingredients:

- 2 1/2 cups all-purpose flour, unbleached
- 1/4 cup old-fashioned rolled oats and more for sprinkling
- 1/4 cup whole wheat flour, unbleached
- 2 tablespoons sesame seeds and more for sprinkling
- 1 1/2 teaspoon salt
- 2 tablespoons pumpkin seeds and more for sprinkling
- 1 tablespoon flaxseeds and more for sprinkling
- 1/2 teaspoon instant yeast
- 1 tablespoon poppy seeds and more for sprinkling
- 1 1/2 cups water, at room temperature

Directions

1. Take a large bowl, place all the flours in it, add oats, salt, all the seeds, and yeast, and then stir until combined.
2. Pour in the water and stir well until well mixed and a chunky dough comes together; add more water if needed.
3. Then cover the bowl with a wrap or a moist cloth and let the prepared dough rest for 12 hours or more.
4. When ready to bake, switch on the oven, set it to 450 degrees F, place a 4 to 6 quarts pot with a lid in it and let it preheat for a minimum of 30 minutes.

5. After 30 minutes, remove the pot from the oven, and line it carefully with a parchment sheet.
6. Remove the dough from the bowl, shape it into a bowl, carefully place it into the prepared pot and then sprinkle seeds on top.
7. Cover the pot with its lid, transfer it to the oven and then bake for 30 minutes.
8. Then uncover the pot, and continue baking the bread for 10 to 15 minutes until the crust turns golden and crisp.
9. When done, transfer the bread to a cooling rack to cool completely and slice to serve.

Nutritional Information Per Serving:

Calories: 118 Cal; Total Fats: 3.4 g; Saturated Fat: 0.4 g; Carbohydrate: 14.4 g; Sugar: 2 g; Fiber: 3 g; Protein: 5.5 g

Rosemary and Olive oil Bread

Preparation Time: 12 hours and 10 minutes | Cooking Time: 45 minutes| Servings: 8

Ingredients:

- 15 ounces of all-purpose flour, unbleached
- 3 tablespoons chopped rosemary
- 1/2 teaspoon instant yeast
- 1 1/2 teaspoon salt
- 1/4 cup olive oil
- 1 1/4 cup water, at room temperature

Directions

1. Take a large bowl, add flour, salt, rosemary, and yeast and stir until just mixed.
2. Pour in oil and water and then stir until incorporated and a wet

and sticky dough comes together.

3. Cover the bowl with a moist towel or a plastic wrap and let the dough rest for 10 to 12 hours at a warm place until covered in bubbles and doubled in size.
4. Sprinkle a clean working space with flour, place dough on it, fold it multiple times, and shape it into a ball.
5. Take a piece of parchment paper, grease it with oil, place the dough on it, cover it with a moist towel and let it rest for another hour.
6. When ready to bake, switch on the oven, set it to 500 degrees F, place a pot with its lid into it and let it preheat for a minimum of 30 minutes.
7. After 30 minutes, make some slits on top of the bread and then place the dough into the pot using parchment paper.
8. Cover the pot with its lid, transfer it to the oven, switch the oven temperature to 425 degrees and then bake for 30 minutes.
9. Then uncover the pot, and continue baking the bread for 10 to 15 minutes until the crust turns golden and crisp.
10. When done, transfer the bread to a cooling rack to cool completely and slice to serve.

Nutritional Information Per Serving:

Calories: 150 Cal; Total Fats: 2.5 g; Saturated Fat: 0.7 g; Carbohydrate: 26 g; Sugar: 0 g; Fiber: 1 g; Protein: 4 g

Italian Breads

Challah

Preparation Time: 2 hours and 45 minutes | Cooking Time: 30 minutes| Servings: 20

Ingredients:

- 1 teaspoon salt
- 2 1/4 teaspoons active dry yeast
- 4 cups all-purpose flour, unbleached
- 1/4 cup sugar
- 6 tablespoons olive oil
- 7 large egg yolks
- 1 cup water, warm
- 1 egg white, at room temperature, beaten
- 2 tablespoons toasted sesame seeds

Directions

1. Take a small bowl, place yeast in it, pour in the warm water, and then stir until combined.
2. Then stir a large pinch of sugar until dissolved and set the mixture aside for 10 minutes until it turns foamy.
3. Then take a large bowl, place flour in it, add salt and sugar, pour in egg yolks and oil, and stir well until well combined.
4. Pour in the yeast mixture and stir until a wet and sticky dough comes together.
5. Sprinkle a clean working space with flour, place dough on it and then knead for 10 minutes until smooth and elastic; knead in more flour until the dough is sticky.
6. Grease the bowl with oil, place the dough in it, cover it with a cloth, place the bowl in a warm place and then let it rest at a warm place for 2 hours or more until doubled in size.
7. Then transfer the dough to a working space, punch it down, divide it into three pieces and then roll each dough piece into a 16-inch-long rope.
8. Now braid all three dough ropes together and when done,

squeeze the ends together.
9. Take a large baking sheet, line it with a parchment sheet, place the braided challah on it, cover it with a cloth, place it in a warm place and let it rest for 30 minutes.
10. Meanwhile, switch on the oven, then set it to 350 degrees F and let it preheat.
11. Then brush the loaf with egg whites, sprinkle with sesame seeds, and then bake for 20 to 25 minutes until cooked and golden brown.
12. When done, let the bread cool on a wire rack at room temperature, cut it into slices, and then serve.

Nutritional Information Per Serving:

Calories: 124 Cal; Total Fats: 6.5 g; Saturated Fat: 1.3 g; Carbohydrate: 22.2 g; Sugar: 1 g; Fiber: 1 g; Protein: 3.9 g

Salty Italian Bread

Preparation Time: 2 hours and 45 minutes | Cooking Time: 20 minutes| Servings: 24

Ingredients:

- 3 1/2 cups bread flour, unbleached
- 1 teaspoon Italian herbs seasoning
- 1 teaspoon sugar
- 2 teaspoons bread machine yeast
- 2 tablespoons olive oil
- 1 teaspoon salt
- 1/8 teaspoon coarse salt
- 1 1/4 cup milk, lukewarm

Directions

1. Plug in a bread machine, add ingredients according to the

manufacturer's instructions, or pour oil and milk into its pan.
2. Add remaining ingredients, reserving coarse salt, select the "dough" or "knead" setting and wait until done.
3. Then sprinkle a clean working space with flour, transfer the prepared dough on it and then shape it into a ball.
4. Take a non-stick baking sheet, place dough on it, brush the top with oil, cover it with a moist towel and let it rest for 1 hour.
5. Then switch on the oven, set it to 450 degrees F and let it preheat.
6. After 1 hour, make 3 diagonal cuts on top of the dough, about ½-inch deep and 4 inches apart, and then sprinkle salt on top.
7. Place the baking sheet containing dough into the oven, and then bake for 17 to 20 minutes until golden.
8. When done, transfer the bread loaf to a wire rack and let it cool completely.
9. When ready to eat, cut the bread loaf into slices and then serve.

Nutritional Information Per Serving:

Calories: 88 Cal; Total Fats: 2 g; Saturated Fat: 1 g; Carbohydrate: 14 g; Sugar: 1 g; Fiber: 1 g; Protein: 3 g

Rosemary and Garlic Focaccia Bread

Preparation Time: 1 hour and 40 minutes | Cooking Time: 20 minutes| Servings: 15

Ingredients:

- 2 1/2 cups all-purpose flour, unbleached
- 1/2 teaspoon sea salt
- 1 tablespoon minced garlic
- 1 teaspoon dried thyme
- 2 1/4 teaspoons active dry yeast
- 1 teaspoon dried rosemary

- 1/4 teaspoon honey
- 1/4 teaspoon ground black pepper
- 1 cup water, warm
- 1/2 cup olive oil

Directions

1. Take a medium skillet pan, place it over low heat, add garlic, thyme, black pepper, and rosemary in it, pour in oil, stir until combined, and cook for 5 to 10 minutes until golden brown, and set aside until required.
2. Take a large bowl, add yeast and honey in it, pour in water, stir until combined, and let the mixture rest for 5 to 10 minutes until foamy.
3. Take a large bowl, place 1 cup flour in it, spoon 1/4 cup of the prepared garlic mixture in it, add yeast mixture, stir until moist mixture comes together, and let it rest for 5 minutes.
4. Then add the remaining flour into the bowl, add salt and then stir until well combined.
5. Transfer the mixture to a clean working space dusted with flour and then knead for 10 to 15 minutes until the smooth and elastic dough comes together.
6. Oil the bowl, place the dough in it, cover it with a moist towel and let it rest in a warm place for 1 hour until doubled in size.
7. When ready to bake, switch on the oven, then set it to 450 degrees F and let it preheat.
8. Take a rimmed baking sheet, about 13-inch, place dough in it, spread it evenly by pressing down with fingers and spread the remaining garlic mixture on top.
9. Place the baking sheet containing dough into the oven and then bake for 15 to 20 minutes until golden brown.
10. When done, transfer the bread loaf to a wire rack and let it cool completely.
11. When ready to eat, cut the bread loaf into pieces and then serve.

Nutritional Information Per Serving:

Calories: 143 Cal; Total Fats: 8 g; Saturated Fat: 2 g; Carbohydrate: 16 g; Sugar: 0 g; Fiber: 1 g; Protein: 3 g

★★★★★

Bread Machine Ciabatta

Preparation Time: 20 minutes | Cooking Time: 1 day and 20 minutes| Servings: 16

Ingredients:

- 3/4 teaspoon bread machine yeast
- 1/2 cup water, at room temperature
- 3 cups all-purpose flour, unbleached, divided
- 1/2 cup water, chilled
- 1/4 cup milk, at room temperature
- 1 1/2 teaspoon salt

Directions

1. Plug in a bread machine, pour water into its pan, and add 1 cup flour and 1/8 teaspoon yeast.
2. Press the "dough" cycle button, press the "start" button, let the mixture mix for 5 minutes, then switch off the bread machine and let the mixture rest for a minimum of 12 hours or 24 hours.
3. Then pour in the remaining water and milk, add the remaining flour and salt, add yeast at the end, press the "dough" cycle button and then press the "start" button.
4. When the cycle end, the dough should be of a pancake consistency, and if not, stir in 1 tablespoon of flour at a time.
5. Take a 3-quarts container, rectangle-shaped, grease it with oil, place dough in it, cover it with a towel, and let it rest for a minimum of 1 hour or until doubled in size.
6. Then lift the dough from the corners and sides to the middle, return the cover on top and let it rest for another 30 minutes.

7. Dust a clean working space with flour, and flip the dough container on it to take out the dough; don't punch it down.
8. Divide the rectangle dough lengthwise in half, and then shape each dough into a ciabatta using well-greased fingers.
9. Transfer the loaves to a large baking sheet, cover them completely with a greased plastic wrap and let them rest for 45 minutes until puffy.
10. Meanwhile, switch on the oven, then set it to 450 degrees F and let it preheat.
11. Spray the loaves with water, place the baking sheet into the oven, and bake for 18 to 20 minutes until the crust turn golden.
12. When done, let the loaves cool down on the wire rack and then serve.

Nutritional Information Per Serving:

Calories: 89 Cal; Total Fats: 1 g; Saturated Fat: 1 g; Carbohydrate: 18 g; Sugar: 1 g; Fiber: 1 g; Protein: 3 g

Pagnotta

Preparation Time: 15 minutes | Cooking Time: 2 hours | Servings: 8

Ingredients:

- 3 1/2 cups white bread flour, unbleached
- 1 teaspoon salt
- 1 tablespoon honey
- 1 teaspoon active yeast
- 1 tablespoon olive oil
- 1 1/4 cup water

Directions

1. Take a large bowl, place flour in it, add salt, yeast, and honey and then stir in water, 1/4 cup at a time, until the dough comes

together.
2. Dust a clean working space with flour, place dough on it and knead it for 10 minutes until elastic and smooth.
3. Take a large bowl, grease it with oil, place dough in it, cover it with a towel, and let it rest for 50 minutes until doubled in size.
4. Transfer the dough to a working space, press the dough gently to shape it into a square, fold the dough edges to the center, and then fold again to shape the dough into a round.
5. Return the dough to the bowl, cover it with a moist towel, and let it rest for a minimum of 20 minutes until doubled in size.
6. Meanwhile, switch on the oven, then set it to 450 degrees F and let it preheat.
7. Take a baking sheet, line it with parchment paper, place dough on it and then bake for 25 to 45 minutes until thoroughly cooked.
8. Let the loaf cool down completely on the wire rack, then cut it into slices and serve.

Nutritional Information Per Serving:

Calories: 140 Cal; Total Fats: 0.5 g; Saturated Fat: 0.5 g; Carbohydrate: 30 g; Sugar: 0 g; Fiber: 1 g; Protein: 4 g

French Breads

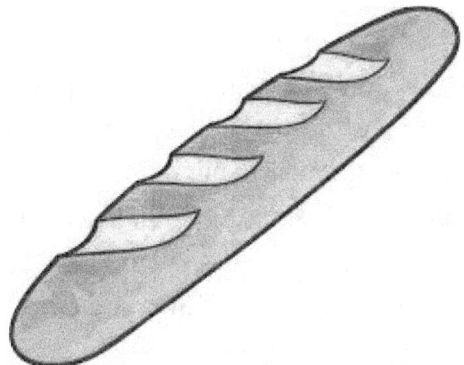

French Baguettes

Preparation Time: 1 hour and 15 minutes | Cooking Time: 25 minutes| Servings: 12

Ingredients:

- 2 1/2 cups bread flour, unbleached
- 1 tablespoon white sugar
- 1 1/2 teaspoon bread machine yeast
- 1 teaspoon salt
- 1 egg yolk
- 1 cup and 1 tablespoon water

Directions

1. Plug in a bread machine, pour in 1 cup water, add flour, salt, sugar, and yeast at the end, press the "dough" cycle button, and then press the "start" button.
2. Take a large bowl, grease it with oil, place dough in it, turn it to coat completely with oil, cover it with a towel and let the dough rest at a minimum of 30 minutes at a warm place until doubled in size.
3. Then transfer the dough to a clean working space dusted with flour, punch it down and then shape it into a 16-by-12-inch rectangle dough.
4. Divide the dough into two rectangles, each about 8-by-12 inches, and then start rolling each dough from the long side.
5. Take a cookie sheet, grease it with oil, place both doughs on it at some distance and then make lengthwise cuts on them every 2 inches.
6. Cover both doughs with a towel, and place them in a warm place for 30 minutes or more until doubled in size.
7. Meanwhile, switch on the oven, then set it to 375 degrees F and let it preheat.
8. Take a small bowl, place egg yolk in it, pour 1 tablespoon of water, and then whisk until blended.

9. Brush the yolk mixture over the loaves and then bake for 20 to 25 minutes until the crust turn golden.
10. When done, let the loaves cool completely on a wire rack, cut them into slices, and then serve.

Nutritional Information Per Serving:

Calories: 113 Cal; Total Fats: 1 g; Saturated Fat: 0 g; Carbohydrate: 22 g; Sugar: 1 g; Fiber: 1 g; Protein: 4 g

Garlic and Herb Bread

Preparation Time: 2 hours and 30 minutes (includes rising time)

Ingredients:
- 3 cups all-purpose flour
- 1 teaspoon salt
- 1 teaspoon dried oregano
- 1 packet of active dry yeast
- 1 1/2 cups warm water
- 2 tablespoons olive oil
- 4 cloves of garlic, minced
- 2 tablespoons chopped fresh herbs (such as basil, rosemary, thyme)

Directions
1. In a large mixing bowl, combine the flour, salt, and oregano.
2. In a separate bowl, dissolve the yeast in warm water. Let stand for 5 minutes until the mixture becomes frothy.
3. Add the yeast mixture, olive oil, garlic, and herbs to the flour mixture and stir until a dough forms.
4. Turn the dough out onto a floured surface and knead for 10 minutes until the dough is smooth and elastic.
5. Place the dough in a lightly oiled bowl, cover with a damp cloth, and let it rise in a warm place for 1 hour.

6. Preheat the oven to 425°F (220°C).
7. Transfer the dough to a greased loaf pan and let it rise for another 30 minutes.
8. Bake the bread in the preheated oven for 30-35 minutes, or until the crust is golden brown.
9. Let the bread cool in the pan for 5 minutes before removing it from the pan and letting it cool completely on a wire rack.

Nutritional Information Per Serving (1 slice):

Calories: 140, Fat: 5 g, Sodium: 220 mg, Carbohydrates: 26 g, Fiber: 1 g, Protein: 4g, Cholesterol: 0 mg, Calcium: 40 mg

Country French Bread

Preparation Time: 5 hours minutes | Cooking Time: 25 minutes | Servings: 8

Ingredients:

- 3/4 cup whole wheat flour, unbleached
- 1 tablespoon salt
- 1 teaspoon instant yeast, divided
- 6 cups bread flour, unbleached
- 3 cups warm water, divided

Directions

1. Take a large bowl, pour in 1/2 cup water, and stir in 1/2 teaspoon yeast and whole-wheat flour until thick batter comes together.
2. Cover the bowl containing batter with a moist kitchen towel and let the mixture rest for a minimum of 2 hours or 8 hours until bubbly, or let the mixture rest for 12 hours in the refrigerator and then bring it to room temperature.
3. Dust the clean working space with flour, transfer the dough on

it and then knead for 10 to 12 minutes until smooth and elastic.
4. Shape the dough into a round, then cover it with a moist cloth, and let it rest for a minimum of 10 minutes.
5. Then take a large bowl, grease it with oil, place the dough in it, turn it to coat in oil, cover the bowl with a moist towel and let it rest for a minimum of 2 hours at room temperature until doubled in size.
6. Then transfer the dough to the working space, punch it down, divide it into two pieces
7. and shape each dough piece into a round.
8. Cover both dough rounds with a moist towel, let them rest for 30 minutes, and then shape each dough piece into a baguette.
9. Dust a cloth heavily with flour, place it on a baking sheet in such a way that it separates the loaves, and then place the prepared loaves on the baking sheet, seam side up.
10. Sprinkle some more flour over the loaves, cover them with a moist towel and let them rest for a minimum of 2 hours until doubled in size.
11. When ready to bake, switch on the oven, then set it to 375 degrees F and let it rest.
12. Take a separate baking sheet, sprinkle it with flour, transfer the loaves on it seam-sidedown, make some cuts on the loaves and then bake for 25 minutes or more until golden brown.
13. Let the bread loaves cool completely on the wire rack and then serve.

Nutritional Information Per Serving:

Calories: 48 Cal; Total Fats: 0 g; Saturated Fat: 0 g; Carbohydrate: 10 g; Sugar: 0 g; Fiber: 2 g; Protein: 2 g

French Spiced Bread

Preparation Time: 20 minutes | Cooking Time: 1 hour| Servings: 10

Ingredients:

- 1 1/4 cup dark rye flour, unbleached
- 1 1/2 teaspoon ground cinnamon
- 1 cup all-purpose flour, unbleached
- 1/4 teaspoon grated nutmeg
- 1 1/2 tablespoon brown sugar
- 1 1/2 teaspoon ground ginger
- 2 whole star anise
- 1/2 teaspoon anise seeds, whole
- 1/4 teaspoon ground cloves
- 1 1/2 teaspoon baking soda
- 1/4 teaspoon ground black pepper
- 1/4 teaspoon salt
- 1 cup milk, at room temperature
- 1/4 teaspoon grated orange zest
- 2/3 cup and 1 tablespoon honey

Directions

1. Switch on the oven, then set it to 305 degrees F and let it preheat.
2. Take a 9-inch loaf pan, grease it with butter, dust it with flour, and then set aside until required.
3. Take a medium saucepan, place it over medium heat, pour in the milk, add stat anise and then whisk in honey until dissolved.
4. Then remove the pan from heat and set aside until required.
5. Take a large bowl, place both flours in it along with sugar, salt, black pepper, baking soda, all the spices, and orange zest and whisk until combined.
6. Slowly stir in the prepared milk mixture until just combined,

using a wooden spoon, and then spoon it into the prepared pan.
7. Place the prepared loaf pan into the oven and then bake for 1 hour until done and an inserted wooden stick into the middle of the loaf comes out clean.
8. When done, let the loaf cool in its pan for 30 minutes, take it out, and then let it cool completely.
9. Cut the loaf into slices and then serve.

Nutritional Information Per Serving:

Calories: 115 Cal; Total Fats: 0.8 g; Saturated Fat: 0 g; Carbohydrate: 25 g; Sugar: 9.7 g; Fiber: 3.5 g; Protein: 1.2 g

★★★★★

Tarte Flambee

Preparation Time: 15 minutes | Cooking Time: 20 minutes | Servings: 2

Ingredients:

- 1 cup all-purpose flour, unbleached
- 1 tablespoon olive oil
- 1/4 teaspoon salt
- 1/4 cup water, at room temperature

For the Topping:

- 1/8 teaspoon ground nutmeg
- 1/2 of a medium onion, peeled, sliced
- 2.5 ounces bacon, cut into strips
- 3 tablespoons crème fraiche, at room temperature
- 1/2 tablespoon butter, unsalted
- 1/2 cup gruyere cheese

Directions

1. Take a medium bowl, place flour in it, add salt, pour in oil and

water, and then stir well until the dough comes together.
2. Dust a clean working space with flour, place dough on it and then knead for 2 to 3 minutes until smooth and elastic.
3. Switch on the oven, then set it to 450 degrees F and let it preheat.
4. Take a large baking sheet, line it with parchment paper, and then set aside until required.
5. Take a small frying pan, place it over medium heat and when hot, add bacon strips and cook until it begins to brown.
6. When done, transfer bacon strips to a plate, add butter and onion to the pan and then cook for 4 to 5 minutes until soft and golden.
7. Take a small bowl, place crème Fraiche in it and then stir in salt, nutmeg, and black pepper until combined.
8. Roll the prepared dough into a 1/8-inch-thick round, transfer it to the baking sheet, and then spread the prepared crème Fraiche mixture on it, leaving some space on the edges.
9. Scatter onions and bacon on top, cover with cheese and then bake for 10 minutes until edges turn crispy and light brown.
10. When done, cut the tart into two sections and then serve.

Nutritional Information Per Serving:

Calories: 512 Cal; Total Fats: 28 g; Saturated Fat: 9 g; Carbohydrate: 52 g; Sugar: 2 g; Fiber: 2 g; Protein: 12 g

★★★★★

Rye Bread

Preparation Time: 1 hour and 30 minutes | Cooking Time: 40 minutes| Servings: 12

Ingredients:

- 2 1/2 cups bread flour, unbleached
- 2 1/4 teaspoons active dry yeast

- 1 cup rye flour, unbleached
- 6 tablespoons molasses
- 1 tablespoon caraway seeds
- 2 tablespoon cocoa powder, unsweetened
- 1/2 tablespoon salt
- 2 tablespoons olive oil
- 1 1/4 cup warm water

Directions

1. Take a large bowl, place water in it, stir in yeast and molasses and let it rest for 10 minutes or until foamy.
2. Add salt, caraway seeds, cocoa powder, and oil, and then stir in rye flour and bread flour, 1/4 cup at a time, until the dough comes together.
3. Dust a clean working surface with flour, place dough on it, and then knead it for 5 to 7 minutes until smooth and elastic; knead more flour if the dough is sticky.
4. Grease the large bowl with oil, place the dough in it, turn it to coat in oil, cover with a moist towel and let the dough rest for a minimum of 1 hour at room temperature until doubled in size.
5. Then lightly press down the dough to release its air, transfer the dough to the dusted working space, knead for 1 minute, divide evenly into two pieces, and then shape each dough section into a loaf.
6. Take a baking sheet, dust it with flour, place both loaves on it, cover with a moist towel and let them rest for 45 minutes until risen.
7. Meanwhile, switch on the oven, then set it to 350 degrees F and let it preheat.
8. Make some cuts on top of each loaf, place them into the oven and bake for 40 to 50 minutes until done.
9. Let the loaves cool completely on the wire rack, then cut them into slices and serve.

Nutritional Information Per Serving:

Calories: 185 Cal; Total Fats: 3 g; Saturated Fat: 0 g; Carbohydrate: 35 g; Sugar: 7 g; Fiber: 2 g; Protein: 5 g

Fruits and Nuts Breads

Bread Machine Banana Bread

Preparation Time: 10 minutes | Cooking Time: 1 hour and 40 minutes| Servings: 12

Ingredients:

- 2 cups all-purpose flour, unbleached
- 1 cup of mashed bananas
- 1 teaspoon baking powder
- 1 cup brown sugar
- 1 teaspoon baking soda
- 1 teaspoon vanilla extract, unsweetened
- 1/2 teaspoon salt
- 2 eggs, at room temperature, beaten
- 1/2 cup chopped walnuts
- 8 tablespoons butter, unsalted, softened

Directions

1. Take a bread machine, add ingredients according to the manufacturer's instructions or place mashed bananas, butter, and eggs in its pan.
2. Add the remaining ingredients, and then insert the pan into the bread machine.
3. Plug in the bread machine, press the setting for "sweet quick bread," set the crust color to "light" or "medium," and then press start and let it bake.
4. When the bread cycle is done, take out the pan and then let the bread loaf rest in the pan for 10 minutes.
5. Then transfer the bread loaf to a wire rack and let it cool completely.
6. When ready to eat, cut the bread loaf into slices and then serve.

Nutritional Information Per Serving:

Calories: 250 Cal; Total Fats: 9 g; Saturated Fat: 5 g; Carbohydrate: 41 g; Sugar: 22 g; Fiber: 1 g; Protein: 3 g

★★★★★

Bread Machine Apple Chunk Bread

Preparation Time: 15 minutes | Cooking Time: 1 hour and 30 minutes| Servings: 8

Ingredients:

- 3 cups bread flour, unbleached
- 1/2 teaspoon ground cinnamon
- 1 1/3 cups diced apples, peeled
- 2 tablespoons sugar
- 2 1/2 teaspoons yeast
- 1/4 cup olive oil
- 1 1/2 teaspoons salt
- 1 cup milk, at room temperature

Directions

1. Take a bread machine, add ingredients according to the manufacturer's instructions except for apple or pour in milk and oil in its pan.
2. Add sugar, cinnamon, salt, and flour, and then insert the pan into the bread machine.
3. Plug in the bread machine, press the setting for "knead," and press the "start" button.
4. When done, add the apples, press the setting for "sweet quick bread," set the crust color to "light" or "medium," and then press start and let it bake.
5. When the bread cycle is done, take out the pan and then let the bread loaf rest in the pan for 10 minutes.
6. Then transfer the bread loaf to a wire rack and let it cool completely.
7. When ready to eat, cut the bread loaf into slices and then serve.

Nutritional Information Per Serving:

Calories: 277.6 Cal; Total Fats: 8.4 g; Saturated Fat: 1.6 g; Carbohydrate: 43.8 g; Sugar: 5.4 g; Fiber: 2.1 g; Protein: 6.3 g

★★★★★

Bread Machine Walnut and Raisin Loaf

Preparation Time: 15 minutes | Cooking Time: 1 hour and 30 minutes| Servings: 8

Ingredients:

- 1 cup whole wheat flour, unbleached
- 1 1/4 teaspoons salt
- 1 1/4 cups bread flour, unbleached
- 1/2 teaspoon ground cinnamon
- 2 tablespoons honey
- 1/3 cup rye flour, unbleached
- 2 tablespoons molasses
- 1 3/4 teaspoon bread machine yeast
- 2 tablespoons olive oil
- 1/3 cup raisins
- 1/4 cup dry milk powder
- 1/2 cup yogurt, at room temperature
- 1/3 cup chopped walnuts
- 2/3 cup water, at room temperature

Directions

1. Take a bread machine, add ingredients according to the manufacturer's instructions except for nuts and raisins, or pour water and yogurt into its pan.
2. Add the remaining ingredients with yeast at the end, reserving nuts and raisins, and then insert the pan into the bread machine.

3. Plug in the bread machine, press the setting for "knead," and press the "start" button.
4. When done, add the apples, press the setting for "sweet quick bread," set the crust color to "light" or "medium," and then press start and let it bake.
5. 5   When the bread cycle is done, take out the pan and then let the bread loaf rest in the pan for 10 minutes.
6. Then transfer the bread loaf to a wire rack and let it cool completely.
7. When ready to eat, cut the bread loaf into slices and then serve.

Nutritional Information Per Serving:

Calories: 273.5 Cal; Total Fats: 7.8 g; Saturated Fat: 1.2 g; Carbohydrate: 45.6 g; Sugar: 13.6 g; Fiber: 3.5 g; Protein: 7.7 g

Cranberry Bread

Preparation Time: 15 minutes | Cooking Time: 1 hour| Servings: 12

Ingredients:

- 12 ounces cranberries, fresh or frozen
- 1 1/2 cups all-purpose flour, unbleached
- 1 cup sugar
- 1 teaspoon baking powder
- 1 teaspoon vanilla extract, unsweetened
- 1/2 teaspoon salt
- 2 eggs, at room temperature
- 3/4 cup milk, at room temperature
- 1/3 cup butter, unsalted, softened

Directions

1. Switch on the oven, then set it to 350 degrees F and let it preheat.

2. Meanwhile, take an 8-by-4 inches loaf pan, grease it with butter, dust it with flour and set aside until required.
3. Take a large bowl, place butter in it, add sugar and then beat for 2 to 3 minutes until fluffy.
4. Then beat in eggs and vanilla until fully combined.
5. Take a separate large bowl, place flour in it, add baking powder, and then stir this mixture into the egg mixture, 1/4 cup at a time, until well combined and incorporated.
6. Stir in cranberries until just mixed, spoon the batter into the pan and then bake for 1 hour until done and inserted toothpick into the bread comes out clean.
7. Let the bread cool in its pan for 10 minutes and then cool completely on the wire rack.
8. Cut the bread into slices and then serve.

Nutritional Information Per Serving:

Calories: 284 Cal; Total Fats: 6 g; Saturated Fat: 3 g; Carbohydrate: 51 g; Sugar: 2 g; Fiber: 1 g; Protein: 4 g

Lemon and Blueberry Bread

Preparation Time: 15 minutes | Cooking Time: 1 hour| Servings: 16

Ingredients:

- 1 cup blueberries, fresh or frozen
- 1 1/2 cups all-purpose flour, unbleached
- 1/2 cup chopped nuts
- 1 teaspoon baking powder
- 1/2 teaspoon salt
- 1/3 cup butter, unsalted, melted
- 1 cup sugar
- 3 tablespoons lemon juice
- 1/2 cup milk, at room temperature

- 2 eggs, at room temperature
- 2 tablespoons grated lemon zest

Directions

1. Switch on the oven, then set it to 350 degrees F and let it preheat.
2. Meanwhile, take a large bowl, crack eggs in it, add sugar, lemon juice, and butter in it and beat until blended.
3. Stir in salt, baking powder, and flour, 1/4 cup at a time, until incorporated, and then stir in berries, lemon zest, and chopped nuts until just mixed.
4. Take an 8-by-4-inch loaf pan, grease it with butter, spoon the batter into it and then bake 1 hour until done and inserted toothpick into the bread comes out clean.
5. Let the bread cool in its pan for 10 minutes and then cool completely on the wire rack.
6. Cut the bread into slices and then serve.

Nutritional Information Per Serving:

Calories: 181 Cal; Total Fats: 7 g; Saturated Fat: 3 g; Carbohydrate: 27 g; Sugar: 17 g; Fiber: 1 g; Protein: 3 g

★★★★★

Sweet Breads

Bread Machine Molasses Bread

Preparation Time: 2 hours and 30 minutes | Cooking Time: 40 minutes| Servings: 10

Ingredients:

- 4 cups bread flour, unbleached
- 1/3 cup molasses
- 2 tablespoons butter, softened, unsalted
- 1 tablespoon active dry yeast
- 2 tablespoons dry milk powder
- 2 teaspoons salt
- 1 5/8 cups water, at room temperature

Directions

1. Take a bread machine, add ingredients according to the manufacturer's instructions, or pour water into its pan.
2. Add the remaining ingredients with yeast at the end, and then insert the pan into the bread machine.
3. Plug in the bread machine, press the setting for "knead," and press the "start" button.
4. Take a 9-by-5 inches loaf pan, grease it with butter and set aside until required.
5. Shape the dough, place it into the prepared bread pan and let it rest for 1 hour or until doubled in size.
6. Then switch on the oven, set it to 350 degrees F and let it preheat.
7. Place the prepared pan into the oven and then bake for 40 minutes until done and inserted toothpick into the bread comes out clean.
8. Let the bread cool in its pan for 10 minutes and then cool completely on the wire rack.
9. Cut the bread into slices and then serve.

Nutritional Information Per Serving:

Calories: 234 Cal; Total Fats: 3 g; Saturated Fat: 2 g; Carbohydrate: 44 g; Sugar: 12 g; Fiber: 1 g; Protein: 7 g

★★★★★

Cinnamon and Sugar Bread

Preparation Time: 15 minutes | Cooking Time: 50 minutes | Servings: 10

Ingredients:

- 2 cups all-purpose flour, unbleached
- 1 1/3 cup white sugar, divided
- 1 tablespoon baking powder
- 1/2 teaspoon salt
- 2 teaspoons ground cinnamon
- 1 egg, at room temperature
- 1/3 cup olive oil
- 1 cup milk, at room temperature

Directions

1. Switch on the oven, then set it to 350 degrees F and let it preheat.
2. Meanwhile, take a 9-by-5-inch loaf pan, grease it with oil and let it aside until required.
3. Take a large bowl, place flour in it, add salt, 1 cup sugar, and baking powder, and stir until just mixed.
4. Pour in the milk and oil, add egg and then whisk until the smooth batter comes together.
5. Spoon half of the prepared batter into the prepared loaf pan, sprinkle with the remaining sugar and cinnamon, and cover with the remaining batter.
6. Place the prepared loaf pan into the oven and then bake for 50

minutes until done and inserted toothpick into the bread comes out clean.
7. Let the bread cool in its pan for 10 minutes and then cool completely on the wire rack.
8. Cut the bread into slices and then serve.

Nutritional Information Per Serving:

Calories: 80 Cal; Total Fats: 1 g; Saturated Fat: 0.1 g; Carbohydrate: 15 g; Sugar: 4 g; Fiber: 1 g; Protein: 2 g

★★★★★

Lemon Cake Bread

Preparation Time: 10 minutes | Cooking Time: 40 minutes | Servings: 10

Ingredients:

- 1 1/2 cups all-purpose flour, unbleached
- 1 tablespoon grated lemon peel
- 1 cup sugar
- 1/2 cup milk, at room temperature
- 1/8 teaspoon salt
- 2 eggs, at room temperature
- 1 teaspoon baking powder
- 1/2 cup of melted butter, unsalted
- 2 tablespoons lemon juice

Directions

1. Take a bread machine, add ingredients according to the manufacturer's instructions or pour milk and crack eggs in its pan.
2. Add the remaining ingredients and then insert the pan into the bread machine.
3. Plug in the bread machine, press the setting for "sweet quick

bread," set the crust color to "light" or "medium," and then press start and let it bake.
4. When the bread cycle is done, take out the pan and then let the bread loaf rest in the pan for 10 minutes.
5. Then transfer the bread loaf to a wire rack and let it cool completely.
6. When ready to eat, cut the bread loaf into slices and then serve.

Nutritional Information Per Serving:

Calories: 180 Cal; Total Fats: 8 g; Saturated Fat: 2 g; Carbohydrate: 24 g; Sugar: 12 g; Fiber: 0 g; Protein: 2 g

★★★★★

Cinnamon Raisin Bread

Preparation Time: 1 hour and 40 minutes | Cooking Time: 45 minutes | Servings: 8

Ingredients:

- 3 cups bread flour, unbleached
- 2 teaspoons instant yeast
- 2/3 cup sugar
- 1 teaspoon salt
- 1/2 teaspoon ground ginger
- 1 teaspoon ground cinnamon
- 1 cup raisins
- 1/8 teaspoon nutmeg
- 3/4 cup milk, warm
- 1/3 cup butter, unsalted, softened
- 1 egg, beaten
- 3/4 cup water, warm

Directions

1. Take a medium bowl, pour in milk and water, add yeast and

sugar, whisk until combined, and then let the mixture rest for 10 minutes until foamy.
2. Take a large bowl, place flour in it, add salt and all the spices and then stir until mixed.
3. Whisk in milk mixture and butter using a stand mixer until well combined and smooth and elastic dough comes together.
4. Cover the bowl containing dough with a plastic wrap or a moist cloth and then let the dough rest for 1 hour until doubled in size.
5. Then transfer the dough to a clean working space dusted with flour, shape it into a rectangle loaf and transfer it to a pan greased lightly with oil.
6. Cover the pan with a moist towel and let the dough rest for 30 minutes.
7. In the meantime, switch on the oven, set it to 350 degrees F, and let it preheat.
8. Then beat the egg, brush it all over the dough and bake for 30 to 45 minutes until done and inserted toothpick into the bread comes out clean.
9. Let the bread cool in its pan for 10 minutes and then cool completely on the wire rack.
10. Cut the bread into slices and then serve.

Nutritional Information Per Serving:

Calories: 389 Cal; Total Fats: 13 g; Saturated Fat: 6 g; Carbohydrate: 63 g; Sugar: 18 g; Fiber: 5 g; Protein: 9 g

★★★★★★

Stollen

Preparation Time: 25 minutes | Cooking Time: 40 minutes| Servings: 4

Ingredients:

- 2 1/4 cups all-purpose flour, unbleached

- 1/2 cup chopped mixed candied fruit
- 1/2 cup sugar
- 1/2 teaspoon lemon zest
- 1 1/2 teaspoons baking powder
- 1/4 teaspoon salt
- 1/2 cup raisins
- 1 teaspoon vanilla extract, unsweetened
- 1/3 cup almonds, slivered, toasted
- 1/2 teaspoon almond extract, unsweetened
- 1 egg, at room temperature
- 7 tablespoons butter, cold, divided
- 1 cup ricotta cheese
- 1 egg yolk, at room temperature
- Confectioners' sugar, as needed

Directions

1. Switch on the oven, then set it to 350 degrees F and let it preheat.
2. Plug in a blender, add flour in it, add salt, baking powder, sugar, and 6 tablespoons butter, and then pulse until the mixture resembles crumbs.
3. Take a small bowl, place egg, extracts, and egg yolk in it, add cheese, raisins, candied fruit, and lemon zest, and whisk until combined.
4. Transfer the blended flour mixture to a large bowl, add the egg mixture and then stir until just mixed.
5. Transfer the dough to a clean working space dusted with flour and then knead for 1 to 2 minutes until smooth.
6. Shape the dough into 10-by8-inch oval-shaped dough, place it on a greased baking sheet and then bake for 40 to 45 minutes until done and golden.
7. When done, melt the remaining 1 tablespoon of butter, brush it over the baked loaf and then let it cool completely on the wire rack.

8. Dust the cooled loaf with the confectioners' sugar, cut it into slices, and then serve.

Nutritional Information Per Serving:

Calories: 284 Cal; Total Fats: 11 g; Saturated Fat: 6 g; Carbohydrate: 41 g; Sugar: 20 g; Fiber: 2 g; Protein: 6 g

★★★★★

Bonus Recipes!
Pizza

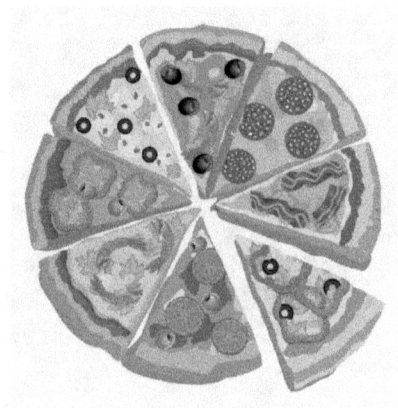

Pepperoni Pizza

Preparation Time: 3 hours and 15 minutes | Cooking Time: 12 minutes | Servings: 8

Ingredients:

For the Dough:

- 4 cups all-purpose flour, unbleached
- 1 1/2 teaspoon instant yeast
- 1 teaspoon olive oil
- 1 1/2 teaspoons salt
- 1 1/2 cups water, lukewarm

For the Topping:

- 1/2 teaspoon ground black pepper
- 20 slices pepperoni
- 1/2 cup pizza sauce
- 1 teaspoon oregano, fresh
- 12 ounces mozzarella cheese, grated

Directions

1. Prepare the dough and for this, place flour into the stand mixer bowl, add then salt and yeast, and whisk at low speed until combined.
2. Pour in the water and continue whisking for 1 to 2 minutes until the dough comes together.
3. Take a large bowl, grease it with oil, place dough in it, turn it to coat with oil, cover the bowl with a moist towel and let it rest for 2 to 3 hours until doubled in size; this will make a 14-inch pizza crust.
4. Switch on the oven, then set it to 500 degrees F and let it preheat.
5. Then transfer the dough to a clean working space dusted with flour, roll it into a 14-inch circle and place it on a large baking

sheet greased with oil.

6. Evenly spread the pizza sauce over the prepared dough, leaving 1/4-inch edges, then cut half of the pepperoni slices into sticks and scatter them over the pizza sauce.
7. Cover with cheese, scatter with remaining pepperoni slices, and then sprinkle with black pepper.
8. Place the prepared pizza into the oven and then bake for 12 minutes until the crust turns golden and the cheese have melted.
9. Cut the pizza into slices and then serve.

Nutritional Information Per Serving:

Calories: 313 Cal; Total Fats: 14 g; Saturated Fat: 6 g; Carbohydrate: 32 g; Sugar: 3 g; Fiber: 1 g; Protein: 15 g

★★★★★

Margherita Pizza

Preparation Time: 3 hours and 15 minutes | Cooking Time: 12 minutes | Servings: 8

Ingredients:

- Pizza dough for the 14-inch crust
- 1/8 teaspoon red pepper flakes
- 1/2 cup sliced cherry tomatoes
- 8 ounces of mozzarella cheese, sliced
- 10 leaves of basil, fresh
- 2 tablespoons olive oil
- 1/2 cup pizza sauce

Directions

1. Follow the instructions of preparing dough from the pepperoni pizza recipe.
2. Then switch on the oven, set it to 500 degrees F and let it

preheat.

3. Meanwhile, transfer the pizza dough to a clean working space dusted with flour, roll it into a 14-inch circle and place it on a large baking sheet greased with oil.
4. Spread the pizza sauce over the dough, leaving 1/4-inch edges, cover with cheese and scatter tomato slices on top.
5. Place the prepared pizza into the oven and then bake for 12 minutes until the crust turns golden and the cheese has melted.
6. When done, sprinkle basil leaves over the pizza, drizzle with olive oil, cut it into slices, and then serve.

Nutritional Information Per Serving:

Calories: 204 Cal; Total Fats: 4 g; Saturated Fat: 1.6 g; Carbohydrate: 34.23 g; Sugar: 0.5 g; Fiber: 1.5 g; Protein: 7.1 g

Red Onions and Mushroom Pizza

Preparation Time: 3 hours and 15 minutes | Cooking Time: 8 minutes | Servings: 8

Ingredients:

- Pizza dough for the 14-inch crust
- 1/3 cup sliced mushrooms
- 1/2 teaspoon salt, and more as needed
- 1/3 cup halved cherry tomatoes
- 1/2 teaspoon ground black pepper, and more as needed
- 1/4 cup sliced red onions
- 1 tablespoon oregano leaves, fresh
- 1/2 cup shredded mozzarella cheese
- 1 tablespoon olive oil, and more for drizzling
- 1 ounce Parmesan cheese, grated

Directions

1. Follow the instructions of preparing dough from the pepperoni pizza recipe.
2. Then switch on the oven, set it to 450 degrees F and let it preheat.
3. Meanwhile, transfer the pizza dough to a clean working space dusted with flour, roll it into a 14-inch circle and place it on a large baking sheet greased with oil.
4. Take a large bowl, place mushrooms, tomatoes, and onion in it, add oil, salt, and black pepper and then toss until mixed.
5. Spread mozzarella cheese over the crust, scatter the vegetables on it, and then season with some more salt and black pepper.
6. Place the prepared pizza into the oven and then bake for 8 minutes until the crust turn golden and the vegetables have cooked.
7. When done, sprinkle oregano leaves and cheese over the pizza, drizzle with olive oil, cut it into slices, and then serve.

Nutritional Information Per Serving:

Calories: 188.8 Cal; Total Fats: 5.2 g; Saturated Fat: 1.2 g; Carbohydrate: 27.7 g; Sugar: 2.3 g; Fiber: 2.6 g; Protein: 4.7 g

Conclusion

In conclusion, baking bread is a wonderful and rewarding experience that allows you to create delicious, fresh bread in the comfort of your own home. With a few basic ingredients, some essential tools, and a bit of time and patience, you can make a wide variety of breads that suit your taste and dietary needs. Whether you choose to use a regular oven or a bread machine, the process of making bread is a journey that connects you with your kitchen and the timeless tradition of bread making. So why not get started today and discover the joys of baking your own bread!

www.ingramcontent.com/pod-product-compliance
Lightning Source LLC
Chambersburg PA
CBHW070334120526
44590CB00017B/2876